Little
Gardener

Activity & Coloring Book

Monica Wellington

Dover Publications, Inc.
Mineola, New York

Little gardeners will enjoy these exciting activity and coloring pages all about flowers, vegetables, and how to grow a garden. As you turn the pages of this book, you will join Sam and Lucy as they set out on a gardening adventure. Help them complete crossword puzzles, mazes, word searches, connect-the-dots, coloring pages, and more—all about planting flowers and vegetables! There is even a journal where you can write about or draw pictures of the things in your own garden. Try to complete all of the activities on your own, but if you get stuck, just turn to the Solutions Section beginning on page 58.

Bibliographical Note

Little Gardener Activity & Coloring Book, first published by Dover Publications, Inc., in 2019, is a selection of activities and coloring pages in a new format from three previously published Dover books by Monica Wellington: *Color & Garden Flowers* (2010); *Color & Garden Vegetables* (2011); and *Color & Garden Activity Book* (2012).

International Standard Book Number

ISBN-13: 978-0-486-83322-4
ISBN-10: 0-486-83322-4

Manufactured in the United States by LSC Communications
83322401   2019
www.doverpublications.com

Lucy and Sam are growing a beautiful garden. Find and circle 10 things they will need to work in their garden. Search for: gloves, watering can, hose, shovel, wheelbarrow, seed packets, garden journal, trowel, weeding fork, and a rake.

There are many sprouts in Lucy and Sam's
garden. It is so much fun having a garden full of
little plants that are growing fast.

But there is also a lot of work to do in the garden.
It needs to be watered, it needs to be weeded.
Lucy and Sam take care of their garden.

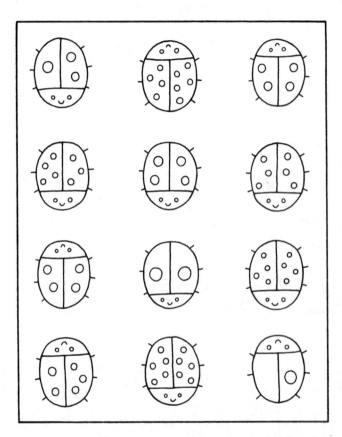

Ladybugs protect garden plants from other harmful
insects. Count the spots on all the ladybug's backs, and
then circle the 3 that have the exact same number.

1. across

1. down

2. across

4. down

5. down

3. across

8. down

7. across

6. down

Use the picture clues to help you
solve the crossword puzzle.

5

glasses

psagre _____

goldfish

trigau _____

giraffe

glove

ogsoe _____

sprpsgaeorh _____

grapes

hgtso _____

asgslse _____

guitar

grasshopper

feigraf _____

toga _____

goat

goose

lsdogihf _____

eovlg _____

ghost

Unscramble each of the 10 words that all
start with the letter G. If you get stuck, the
pictures on the sides of the page are clues!

Now that you have unscrambled 10 things that
begin with the letter G, see if you can find and
circle them hidden in the picture above. You can
use the picture clues on page 6 if you need a hint!

Add color to the little birds and their garden!

Sam picks the first big red ripe tomato.
Lucy pulls up the first big orange carrot.

Lucy and Sam put up a fence so that the hungry
rabbits can't eat the lettuce and carrots.
Keep those hungry rabbits out!

Lucy and Sam make a scarecrow in their garden
with a wood frame and old clothes. They stuff it
with straw. Scare those greedy birds away!

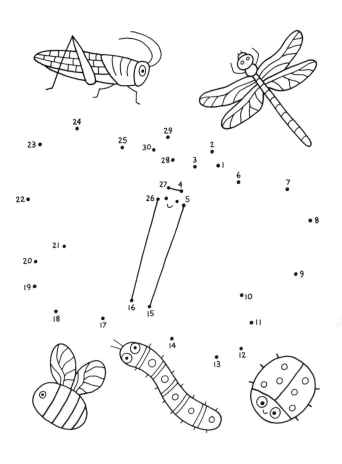

Who is the brightest creature in Sam and Lucy's garden? Connect the dots from 1 to 30 to find out!

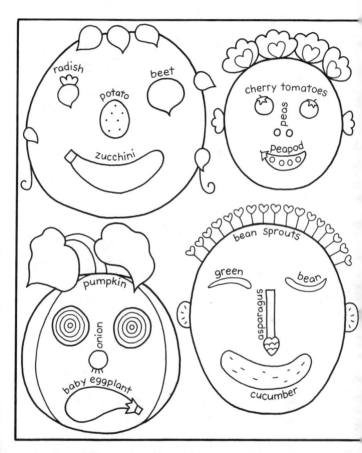

Vegetables come in many shapes and sizes and colors. They can be arranged to make funny faces!

asparagus

peas

lima beans

tomato

scallion onion

cherry tomatoes

lettuce

broccoli

corn

onion

cucumber

bean

pepper

radish

Can you make some funny faces, too?

Lucy and Sam are very excited
when the first flowers bloom.

Their garden is beautiful and filled
with such sweet smells!

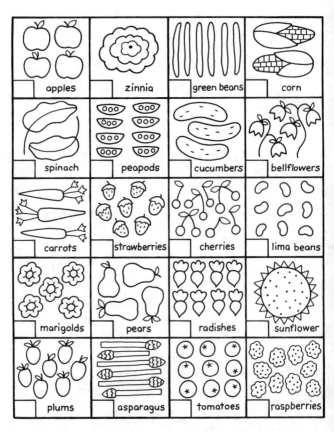

| | apples | | zinnia | | green beans | | corn |

| | spinach | | peapods | | cucumbers | | bellflowers |

| | carrots | | strawberries | | cherries | | lima beans |

| | marigolds | | pears | | radishes | | sunflower |

| | plums | | asparagus | | tomatoes | | raspberries |

Count the number of fruits, vegetables, or
flowers in each square. Then write the correct
numbers in the space provided.

(4)	apples	🍎
+ (4)	pears	🍐
(8)	FRUITS	

( )	marigolds	
+ ( )	bellflowers	
( )	FLOWERS	

( )	asparagus	
+ ( )	green beans	
( )	VEGETABLES	

( )	raspberries	
+ ( )	cherries	
( )	FRUITS	

( )	zinnia	
+ ( )	sunflower	
( )	FLOWERS	

( )	cucumbers	
+ ( )	carrots	
( )	VEGETABLES	

Use the activity on the previous page to fill in the correct number next to the name of each fruit, vegetable, or flower. Then, see if you can solve the math problems!

Find and circle 10 beautiful butterflies in this picture of Sam and Lucy's garden. Then have fun coloring the rest of the picture.

Here is a design of birds, bumblebees, butterflies, and flowers—all things you might find in a garden. Add color to the design.

Color the butterflies with different colors and patterns.

apple

cherry

pear

apricot

peach

plum

Sam and Lucy have many different kinds of fruit trees in their garden. Count how many fruits are in each tree, and then write the correct number in the spaces provided.

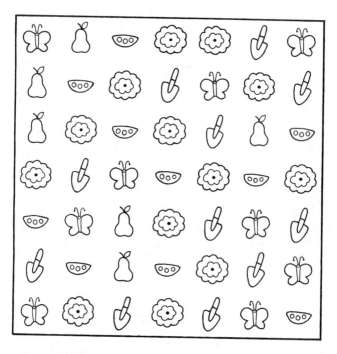

On top of this page is a pattern of garden items that Sam and Lucy have in their garden. Look carefully at the puzzle, and circle the sets of pictures that match the pattern exactly. There are three sets in all. Look down and across.

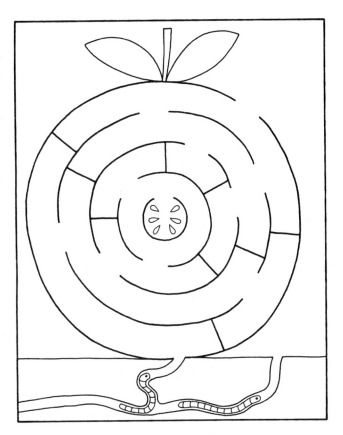

An apple has fallen off a tree. Two worms want to eat their way into the center of the apple, but only one of them will find the way! Try to solve the maze beginning at each worm, and see who makes it to the center.

Lucy and Sam are studying bugs. Can you find all of the following words that describe bugs hidden in the garden? INSECT, WIGGLE, SQUASH, CREEPY, CRAWLY, CREATURES, CHEW, BITE, YUCKY, and BUZZ.

rain + bow = rainbow

sun + flower = _____

butter + (bee/fly) = _____

tiger + (lily) = _____

house + fly = _____

dragon + fly = _____

Use the clues to help you put together
some garden words! The first one has
been done for you to get you started.

bird

butterfly

dragonfly

spider

ladybug

worm

snail

dog

squirrel

rabbit

a	s	p	i	d	e	r	s
b	c	e	g	o	r	t	q
u	b	i	r	d	v	x	u
t	d	l	i	r	y	r	i
t	f	a	l	a	d	a	r
e	h	d	o	g	c	b	r
r	j	y	m	o	f	b	e
f	w	b	s	n	a	i	l
l	o	u	n	f	s	t	z
y	r	g	p	l	u	d	j
b	m	k	q	y	w	k	x

Find and circle the names of these 10 backyard creatures that are hidden in the crossword puzzle above. Look down and across.

All 10 of the creatures listed on the previous
page are hiding in Sam and Lucy's garden!
Find and circle all of them.

Ripe vegetables are ready to pick. What a
harvest! Lucy and Sam are so proud.

Draw the snack that Sam and Lucy made from the
fresh fruits and vegetables they grew in their garden.

They cook a delicious soup and make a big fresh
salad with the vegetables from their garden.

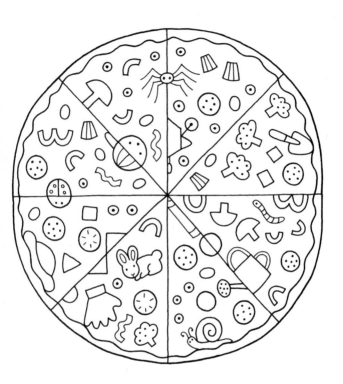

Sam and Lucy made a pizza topped with veggies they grew in their garden. But some things on this pizza you might not want to eat! Find and circle a spider, worm, glove, rabbit, cap, pencil, ladybug, trowel, watering can, hat, snail, and wheelbarrow.

Sam and Lucy and their friends
love growing vegetables!

today

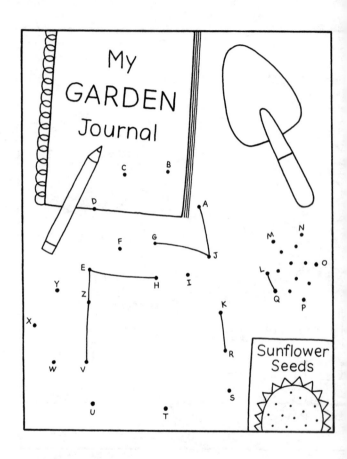

Connect the dots from A to Z to see what important garden tool you need to help your plants grow quickly.

Use the color **green** to color all the shapes with any letter from the word GREEN (**G, R, E, or N**) inside them. You will discover an earth-friendly message about gardens.

Look carefully at these two pictures
of Sam and Lucy's garden.

Circle the 15 things in this picture that make
it different from the one on the left.

Lucy and Sam's garden grows and
grows in the warm summer weather.

It is full of blossoming flowers.

My Garden Journal

. . . .

Now you can keep your very own
Garden Journal just like Sam and Lucy!
A Garden Journal is your own personal
diary where you can record pictures and
facts about the different plants in your
garden. You can record the weather,
the things you did while taking care of
your plants, and other observations.
The best thing about a Garden Journal
is that it will help you remember all the
things you did to take care of your plants,
and all the things that worked the best—
so you can do them again next spring when
it's time to garden again. The pages in this
book will give you an idea of where to start.
After you finish them, you can continue
your Garden Journal by asking an adult to
make some photocopies of the pages for
you and then keep them in a folder or
a loose leaf notebook, or create new
pages by designing them yourself.

Draw or paste a picture of your favorite plants, insects, birds, or other wildlife that you saw in your garden today.

Date: _____

Weather: _____

In the garden today, I....

My favorite thing I saw in the garden today was....

Things to do....

Draw or paste a picture of your favorite plants, insects, birds, or other wildlife that you saw in your garden today.

Date: _____

Weather: _____

In the garden today, I....

My favorite thing I saw in the garden today was....

Things to do....

46

Draw or paste a picture of your favorite plants, insects, birds, or other wildlife that you saw in your garden today.

Date: _____

Weather: _____

In the garden today, I....

My favorite thing I saw in the garden today was....

Things to do....

Draw or paste a picture of your favorite plants, insects, birds, or other wildlife that you saw in your garden today.

Date: _____

Weather: _____

In the garden today, I....

My favorite thing I saw in the garden today was....

Things to do....

Draw or paste a picture of your favorite plants, insects, birds,
or other wildlife that you saw in your garden today.

Date: _____

Weather: _____

In the garden today, I….

My favorite thing I saw in the garden today was….

Things to do….

Draw or paste a picture of your favorite plants, insects, birds, or other wildlife that you saw in your garden today.

Date: _____

Weather: _____

In the garden today, I....

My favorite thing I saw in the garden today was....

Things to do....

Draw or paste a picture of your favorite plants, insects, birds, or other wildlife that you saw in your garden today.

Date: _____

Weather: _____

In the garden today, I....

My favorite thing I saw in the garden today was....

Things to do....

Draw or paste a picture of your favorite plants, insects, birds, or other wildlife that you saw in your garden today.

Solutions

page 1

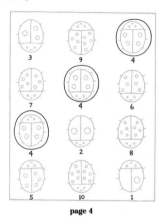

3	9	4
7	4	6
4	2	8
5	10	1

page 4

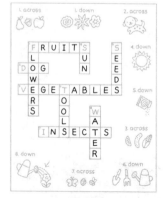

1. across 1. down 2. across
4. down
3. across
5. down
6. down
7. across
8. down

```
    F R U I T S       S
    L       U         E
D O G       N         E
W                     D
E   V E G E T A B L E S
R       O
S       O       W
        L   I N S E C T S
                A
                T
                E
                R
```

page 5

glasses	psagre **grapes**	goldfish
	trigau **guitar**	
	ogsoe **goose**	giraffe
glove	sprpsgaeorh **grasshopper**	
	hgtso **ghost**	
grapes	asgslse **glasses**	guitar
	feigraf **giraffe**	
grasshopper	toga **goat**	goat
	lsdogihf **goldfish**	
goose	eovlg **glove**	ghost

page 6

page 7

page 13

page 18

4 apples	1 zinnia	6 green beans	2 corn
2 spinach	8 peapods	3 cucumbers	5 bellflowers
3 carrots	7 strawberries	10 cherries	9 lima beans
5 marigolds	4 pears	8 radishes	1 sunflower
7 plums	6 asparagus	9 tomatoes	10 raspberries

4 apples + 4 pears = 8 FRUITS	5 marigolds + 5 bellflowers = 10 FLOWERS
6 asparagus + 6 green beans = 12 VEGETABLES	10 raspberries + 10 cherries = 20 FRUITS
1 zinnia + 1 sunflower = 2 FLOWERS	3 cucumbers + 3 carrots = 6 VEGETABLES

page 19

page 20

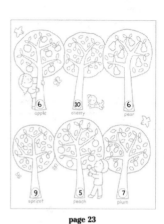

page 23

page 24

page 25

page 26

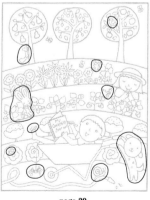

🌧️	+ 🎀	=	rainbow
☀️	+ 🌸	=	sunflower
BUTTER	+ 🧤	=	butterfly
🐱	+ 🌸	=	tigerlily
🏠	+ 💚	=	housefly
🐉	+ 🦋	=	dragonfly

page 27

bird
butterfly
dragonfly
spider

ladybug

worm

snail

dog
squirrel
rabbit

a	s	p	i	d	e	r	t
u	b	i	r	d	v	x	u
t	d	j	i	y	p	y	n
t	f	a	l	a	d	b	r
e	h	o	c	b	r	w	j
r	j	m	o	f	b	e	s
f	v	r	o	s	r	z	n
l	q	p	l	u	d	j	a
y	b	k	g	w	k	x	i
b	k	k	q	w	k	x	i

page 28

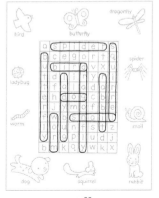

page 29

61

page 33

page 36

page 37

page 39